First published in Great Britain in 2020 by Red Shed,
an imprint of Egmont UK Ltd
2 Minster Court, London EC3R 7BB
www.egmont.co.uk

Text by Clive Gifford
Illustrations by Chris Dickason

ISBN 978 1 4052 9766 0

A CIP catalogue is available from the British Library

Clive Gifford   Chris Dickason

FAKE NEWS

★ ★ ★ ★ ★

★ ★ ★ ★ ★

TRUE OR FALSE?
QUIZ BOOK

RED
SHED

Every day we get an amazing amount of information – pinging at us from websites, TV,

our friends and anywhere else we might look. Some of it sounds incredible. Is it fake? Is it a hoax? Is it just plain wrong … or could it be TRUE? How do you spot the truth from the lies?

In this book you'll find dozens of incredible-sounding facts. They sound pretty unbelievable. But are they false, or are they facts? For example, can it really be true that a fully grown adult reindeer lived all cramped on a World War II submarine for six weeks? What do you think? Amazing but true, or a fake news fib? Just turn the page to find out, and prepare to be amazed!

An adult reindeer lived on a World War II Submarine for six weeks.

TRUE or FALSE?

TRUE! An adult reindeer did live on a World War II submarine for six weeks!

It's rude to turn down a gift – especially from foreign forces fighting on your side in wartime. So in 1941 the captain of British submarine HMS *Trident* had little choice but to accept a present from the Soviet navy. The gift, though, was a fully grown reindeer! The reindeer, named Pollyanna, stayed on board whilst the submarine cruised underwater. She slept alongside the captain, ate her way through a barrel of moss and was fed leftovers. She also developed a liking for tinned condensed milk.

When the submarine finally sailed home to England, Pollyanna went to live at London Zoo.

More than half the cells in your body aren't human.
TRUE or FALSE?

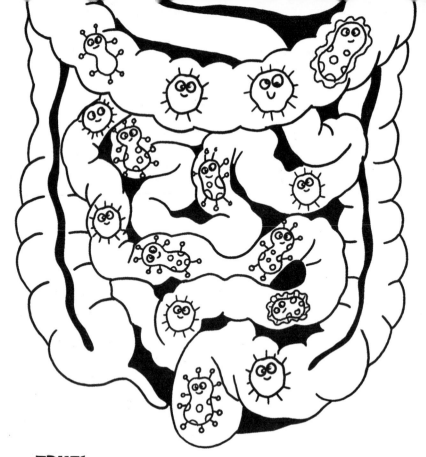

TRUE! More than half the cells in your body aren't human.

Scientists believe that human-body cells only make up somewhere between 10 and 43 per cent of all the cells in your body. They are outnumbered by the billions and trillions of bacteria, fungi, viruses and microscopic creatures that call YOU their home.

Your digestive system is home to fungi such as *Candida* yeasts, as well as trillions of bacteria. Some are harmful and may lead to infections or other health problems, but many bacteria are handy helpers. They aid you in digesting your food and help take out all the nutrients from it. This gives your body energy and the materials and substances it needs to stay healthy.

The Canary Islands are named after canaries.
TRUE or FALSE?

Sliced bread was once banned in the USA.
TRUE or FALSE?

FALSE! The Canary Islands are NOT named after canaries.

Lying off the coast of North Africa, the Canary Islands are popular holiday hotspots, but surprisingly they were not named after the small yellow birds. In fact, the birds were named after the islands.

The islands were called *Canariae Insulae* by the Romans, which means 'the islands of the dogs' in Latin – possibly after wild dogs were spotted on the islands by ancient sailors.

TRUE! Sliced bread was once banned in the USA. In 1943, during World War II, the US War Foods Administration banned the sale of sliced bread. The aim was to save resources, including the thick waxed paper used to hold the slices of the loaf together at the time. Uncut bread also takes a little longer to go stale. Many people were outraged and complained before the ban was lifted just two months later.

A man with a wooden leg won six Olympic medals in a single day.
TRUE or FALSE?

Lightning never strikes the same place twice.
TRUE or FALSE?

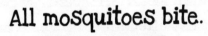

All mosquitoes bite.
TRUE or FALSE?

TRUE! A man with a wooden leg won six Olympic medals in a single day.

A wooden leg didn't stop gymnast George Eyser taking part in the 1904 Olympic Games in the US city of St Louis. He won gold medals in the parallel bars, vault and rope-climbing events, silver in the pommel horse and a bronze on the horizontal bar.

FALSE! Lightning DOES strike the same place twice.

Lightning is more likely to strike prominent objects that are conductive to electricity. The Empire State Building in New York City, USA, is struck by lightning between 25 and 100 times each year.

FALSE! Not all mosquitoes bite.

Male mosquitoes cannot bite at all and only some female mosquitoes do. And even they don't actually bite as they have no jaws. They pierce your skin with a pointed mouthpart called a proboscis.

A day on the planet Venus is longer than its year.

TRUE or FALSE?

Charles Lindbergh was the first person to fly non-stop across the Atlantic Ocean.

TRUE or FALSE?

Spirit of St Louis

TRUE! A day on the planet Venus is longer than its year.

Days on Earth last one-365.25th of an Earth year, but days and years are different on other planets. A day on Jupiter only lasts ten hours, whilst a year on Neptune lasts 165 years! Venus takes 225 Earth days to travel round the Sun – its year. However, it spins really, really slowly and takes 243 Earth days to complete an entire 360-degree turn – its day.

FALSE! Charles Lindbergh was NOT the first person to fly non-stop across the Atlantic Ocean. In 1927, the *Spirit of St Louis* aircraft, piloted by Charles Lindbergh, landed at Le Bourget Aerodrome in France, 33.5 hours after taking off from New York. Lindbergh was the first *solo* aviator to cross the Atlantic non-stop, but the first to cross it non-stop were British airmen John Alcock and Arthur Brown eight years earlier.

A piece of paper cannot be folded more than seven times.
TRUE or FALSE?

FALSE! A piece of paper CAN be folded more than seven times.

Ever tried this yourself? Folding the paper in half the first three or four times is easy, but each time you fold the paper, the number of layers double. So, by the time you make your fifth fold, you have 32 layers to fold, then 64 layers.

After this number of folds, the fibres that make up the paper do not have the flexibility to bend easily, so folding further becomes incredibly hard work.

People believed that no more than seven folds were possible until in 2002 American high-school student Britney Gallivan managed to fold a piece of paper in half an incredible 12 times. Britney used a really long piece of commercial toilet-roll paper that was 1,219 metres long. She folded the paper in half in the same direction each time to achieve her record-breaking feat.

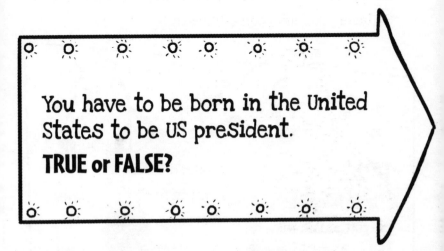

You have to be born in the United States to be US president.
TRUE or FALSE?

The BBC once reported, 'There is no news today' and played music instead.
TRUE or FALSE?

FALSE! You do NOT have to be born in the United States to be US president.

To run for US president, you have to be at least 35 years of age, a US citizen and to have been living in the USA for at least 14 years, but you don't have to be have been born there.

TRUE! The BBC once reported, 'There is no news today' and played music instead.

On 18 April 1930 listeners were surprised to hear the words, 'Good evening. Today is Good Friday. There is no news.' The rest of the 15-minute bulletin was filled with piano music.

You only use
10 per cent
of your brain.
TRUE or FALSE?

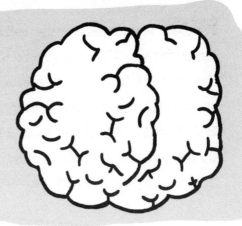

Centipedes have 100 legs.
TRUE or FALSE?

It is illegal to build
sandcastles on
some beaches.
TRUE or FALSE?

FALSE! You do NOT only use 10 per cent of your brain.

Brain scans have revealed that your brain stays active 24/7, even when you're sleeping. Many different parts of your brain are active when you perform tasks, and scientists think that over the course of a day you use almost every part of it.

FALSE! Centipedes NEVER have 100 legs.

'Cent' means 100, but no centipede has 100 legs. It can't, because all centipedes have an odd number of pairs of legs and 50 is an even number. Some of the thousands of centipede species have as few

 as 30 legs whilst some can grow more than 350!

TRUE! It is illegal to build sandcastles on some beaches.

It's against the law to build sandcastles on the beach at Eraclea near the Italian city of Venice. Sandcastle makers also face a fine of up to 150 euros on some beaches at Benidorm in Spain.

A shark once leapt out of the water to attack a helicopter. **TRUE or FALSE?**

FALSE! A shark did NOT leap out of the water to attack a helicopter.

In 2001, an amazing photo went viral on the Internet. It showed a great white shark leaping out of the water to attack a US military helicopter. The message with the photo claimed that the picture had been awarded Photo of the Year by *National Geographic* magazine.

Thousands of people shared the photograph and it appeared on hundreds of website pages worldwide, but it turned out to be a hoax! Someone had merged two real photos, one of the helicopter performing training manoeuvres in San Francisco, USA, and one of a great white shark leaping out of the water off the coast of South Africa in a place named – aptly – False Bay.

'Helicopter Shark' is far from the only photo fake found on the Internet. In 2013, it snowed in Egypt for the first time in over 110 years. An image of the ancient Egyptian Great Sphinx statue covered in snow started whizzing around the world. But the photo was not of the real Sphinx in Egypt but a tiny model version found in a theme park in Japan!

A man once ate an entire aircraft.
TRUE or FALSE?

TRUE! A man once ate an entire aircraft.

Between 1978 and 1980 Frenchman Michel Lotito ate a whole Cessna 150 light aircraft! Nicknamed Monsieur Mangetout (Mr Eat-Everything), he had parts of the plane cut into bite-sized pieces, then gobbled them down. During his metal-munching career, Lotito also ate metal beds, bicycles and a set of skis.

The long jump for horses was once an Olympic sport.
TRUE or FALSE?

Some turtles breathe through their bottoms and wee out of their mouths. **TRUE or FALSE?**

TRUE! The long jump for horses was once an Olympic sport.

The 1900 Olympic Games in Paris, France, featured some strange events, including tug of war, croquet and the standing long jump for humans. It also featured a long-jump competition for horses. The gold medal-winning horse, Extra Dry, managed a jump of 6.10m, which was 107.5cm less than the gold medal-winning human long jump.

TRUE! Some turtles breathe through their bottoms and wee out of their mouths.

In 2012, researchers found that the Chinese soft-shelled turtle actually wees out of both its rear end and its mouth – the only creature known to do so. Other turtles use their backside to obtain oxygen when they are resting or hibernating.

There are trees growing on Earth that have been to the Moon.

TRUE or FALSE?

TRUE! There are trees growing on Earth that have been to the Moon.

The Apollo 14 mission featured several notable firsts. One of the astronauts it carried in 1971, Alan Shepard, became the first and only person to play golf on the Moon! Another of its astronauts, Stuart Roosa, orbited the Moon 34 times.

As a teenager, Roosa had worked in forestry as a smoke jumper, parachuting into remote areas to tackle forest fires before they got out of hand. Roosa helped protect certain tree species and around 500 of their seeds were carried on board Apollo 14 as an experiment. Scientists wondered whether they would still be able to grow after exposure to the conditions in space.

Back on Earth, many of the seeds germinated and around 400 healthy trees grew. These 'Moon trees' were donated all around the world. Records were lost, though, so the whereabouts of some of these special trees is a mystery!

SOS stands for 'Save Our Ship'.
TRUE or FALSE?

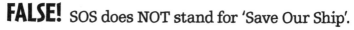

FALSE! SOS does NOT stand for 'Save Our Ship'.

Morse code is used by radio operators to replace letters. It is a 'language' made up of dots and dashes. Three dots, three dashes then three more dots equals SOS – the message of distress sent by sinking ships. It was agreed at a radio conference in 1905, but the letters do not stand for 'Save Our Ship' or 'Save Our Souls'. In fact, it means nothing!

Peanuts are nuts.
TRUE or FALSE?

There's a species of bacteria that only lives in hairspray.
TRUE or FALSE?

A heavy-metal band has a parrot as its lead singer.
TRUE or FALSE?

TRUE! Peanuts are NOT nuts.

True nuts, such as pecans and hazelnuts, grow above ground on trees. Peanuts grow in pods underground and are considered a legume – a group that includes beans and chickpeas.

TRUE! There's a species of bacteria that only lives in hairspray.

In 2008, scientists in Japan discovered a tiny rod-shaped bacteria, which they named *Microbacterium hatanonis*. It has only been found living in hairspray.

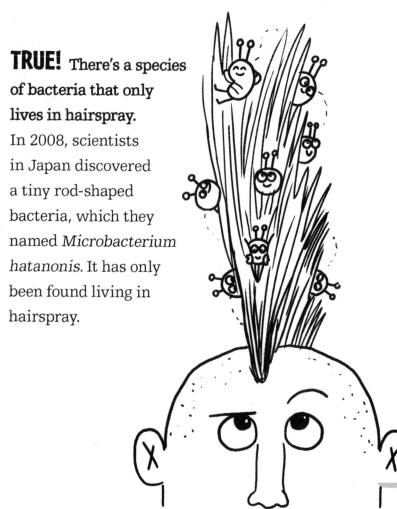

TRUE! A heavy-metal band has a parrot as its lead singer.

Hatebeak were a heavy-metal band formed in 2003 by Blake Harrison and Mark Sloan with a grey parrot called Waldo doing all the 'singing'. In 2015, they released a new album of extremely noisy metal songs called *The Number of the Beak*!

Clouds weigh next to nothing.
TRUE or FALSE?

Farts in jars were used to cure plague victims.
TRUE or FALSE?

FALSE! Clouds do NOT weigh next to nothing.

Those fluffy puffs in the sky look lighter than light. A cloud may hold just a few grams of water vapour in each cubic metre, but if it's huge, it all adds up. According to the UK's Meteorological Office, a typical storm cloud (cumulonimbus) can weigh over 400,000kg. That's the weight of 57 *T. rex* dinosaurs!

TRUE! Farts in jars were used to cure plague victims.

They were used, but not successfully! In the 1600s people thought that life-threatening diseases, such as the plague, were caused by something called miasma, meaning 'bad air'. Some doctors believed that the way to tackle miasma was to dilute it with something else and asked people to collect their farts in glass jars.

A penny dropped from the top of a skyscraper can kill someone on the ground.
TRUE or FALSE?

Captain Cook discovered Australia.
TRUE or FALSE?

FALSE! A penny dropped from the top of a skyscraper can NOT kill someone on the ground.

This often-repeated false fact sounds like it could be correct, but it doesn't allow for something called terminal velocity. When an object falls, drawn back to the Earth's surface by our planet's gravity, it reaches a maximum speed (terminal velocity) due to the resistance it encounters falling through the air. With its two flat sides pushing through air as it falls, a coin does not fall fast – typically well under 100 km per hour. A UK penny or a US cent, even travelling at tens of kilometres per hour, would do little more than sting you.

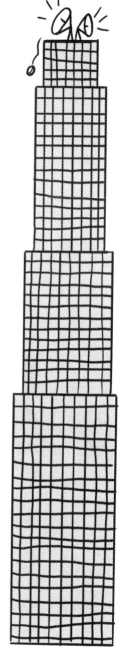

FALSE! Captain Cook did NOT discover Australia.

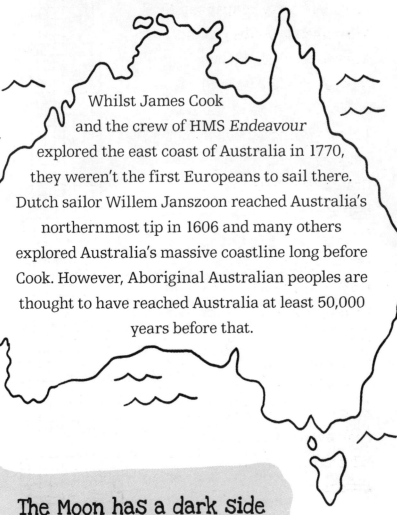

Whilst James Cook and the crew of HMS *Endeavour* explored the east coast of Australia in 1770, they weren't the first Europeans to sail there. Dutch sailor Willem Janszoon reached Australia's northernmost tip in 1606 and many others explored Australia's massive coastline long before Cook. However, Aboriginal Australian peoples are thought to have reached Australia at least 50,000 years before that.

The Moon has a dark side and no gravity.
TRUE or FALSE?

FALSE! The Moon does
NOT have a dark side or zero gravity.

The Moon has a special relationship with Earth.
The pull of gravity keeps it in orbit round our
planet about 384,400km away. The Moon spins
round at the same rate as Earth turns. Scientists
call this being 'tidally locked'. This means that it
always presents the same side of itself to Earth.
People have wondered about the mysterious far
side of the Moon, but it is certainly not dark all
the time. As it spins it receives its share of light
from the Sun – a fact that orbiting space probes
and astronauts in Apollo missions whizzing round
the Moon saw for themselves.

The Apollo missions between 1969 and 1972 carried a total of 12 astronauts on to the Moon. If the Moon had no gravity at all, then the astronauts and their spacecraft wouldn't have stayed on the lunar surface – they would have drifted off into space.

The Moon has about one-sixth of the gravity of Earth, but this gravity pulls on our planet, helping to create the tides in our seas and oceans.

Camels store water in their humps.
TRUE or FALSE?

FALSE! Camels do NOT store water in their humps.

Camels store fat in their humps for times when food is really scarce. They store up to 35 kilograms, which is more than the weight of a typical nine-year-old child! A camel can go many weeks without eating, during which time the fat may get used up and the humps start to droop as a result.

Living in water-scarce surroundings, camels are big drinkers when they get the chance. They can guzzle down over 100 litres of water in 15 minutes. They also have oval-shaped blood cells (humans have round ones) that help the cells pass through their blood vessels when the camel is dehydrated and its blood thickens.

Speaking of camels, which country in the world contains the most? The African nation of Somalia is thought to contain around 6 million, but the biggest herds in the world are found in Australia, which is home to 1–1.2 million wild camels.

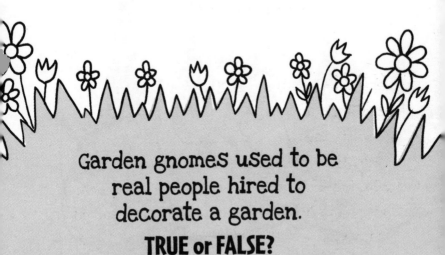

Garden gnomes used to be real people hired to decorate a garden.
TRUE or FALSE?

TRUE! Garden gnomes used to be real people hired to decorate a garden.

In the 17th and 18th century, it was fashionable if you were a rich person to employ someone to live in your gardens. These people were known as ornamental hermits and were given a small hut to live in called a hermitage. They were often asked by their employers to dress in strange clothing, pose in the gardens all day, and never speak to anyone.

Crushed-up Egyptian mummies were used in paintings and drunk as a health cure.

TRUE or FALSE?

TRUE! Crushed-up Egyptian mummies were used in paintings and drunk as a health cure.

The ancient Egyptians were masters at making mummies to preserve the bodies of dead people, and they also mummified animals such as crocodiles, cats, baboons and birds.

By the 16th century there was a growing trade in digging up old mummies in Egypt and shipping them to Europe. Some were ground up to make a powder called mummia, which was mixed with other ingredients to make health remedies. Doctors recommended patients ate or drank mummia to help cure all sorts of health problems – from stomach ulcers to shortness of breath. Famous English scientists Francis Bacon and Robert Boyle praised ground-up mummy for treating bruises and stopping bleeding.

More ground-up mummies were used to make a rich brown paint. 'Mummy brown' was in demand for a while – although some artists used the paint without knowing its gruesome history!

The Vikings wore horned helmets.
TRUE or FALSE?

The man who made Frisbees popular is now a Frisbee.

TRUE or FALSE?

FALSE! The Vikings did NOT wear horned helmets. They really didn't. Dozens of Viking helmets have been discovered by archaeologists and none have horns. Nor were all Vikings bloodthirsty invaders. Most lived in peace at home as farmers, whilst some sailed around Europe to trade with other peoples.

TRUE! The man who made Frisbees popular is now a Frisbee.

Walter Fred Morrison invented plastic flying discs in the 1940s, but things really got flying along in the 1960s when they were relaunched with a new name – the Frisbee. Marketing man 'Steady' Ed Headrick redesigned the Frisbee to make it more stable in flight and founded the International Frisbee Association to organise tournaments.

When Headrick died in 2002 his ashes were mixed with plastic to make a number of memorial Frisbees.

Scottish voters chose the Loch Ness Monster as their national animal.
TRUE or FALSE?

FALSE! Scottish voters did NOT choose the Loch Ness Monster as their national animal. Scotland's national animal has been the unicorn for many centuries. It featured on flags 800 years ago!

Frankenstein was a monster.
TRUE or FALSE?

Some people's sweat is coloured bright yellow, blue or green.
TRUE or FALSE?

It takes 12 bees their whole life to produce a single teaspoon of honey.
TRUE or FALSE?

TRUE! Some people's sweat is coloured bright yellow, blue or green.

Amazingly this is true. In a rare medical condition called chromhidrosis, a chemical called lipofuscin builds up in a person's sweat glands and causes the coloured sweat.

TRUE! It takes 12 bees their whole life to produce a single teaspoon of honey.

Bees are busy workers, buzzing from flower to flower to collect nectar and take it back to their hives to make into honey. Each bee visits 40 to 100 flowers per trip and can fly at speeds up to 25km per hour. It can take visits to over four million flowers to make one kilogram of honey, requiring around 316,000km of flights – enough to circle the world almost eight times!

HELLO
MY NAME IS

FALSE! Frankenstein was NOT a monster. In the book *Frankenstein* by Mary Shelley Victor Frankenstein is the name of the scientist who created the famous monster – not the monster himself. The monster is not even given a name.

Mount Everest is the tallest mountain.

TRUE or FALSE?

FALSE! Mount Everest is NOT the tallest mountain.

Mount Everest, in Asia's mighty Himalayas, stands a whopping 8,850m above sea level, making it the highest-altitude mountain on Earth.

But if we judge a mountain on its height from its base to its peak, then Mauna Kea in Hawaii easily trumps Everest. It may not seem all that high, only reaching an altitude of 4,207.3m at its summit, but the real story lies beneath the ocean's surface. The rest of this mountain extends around 6,000m down to the ocean floor, making the entire mountain over 1,000m taller than Everest.

But those are just high-risers on Earth. Elsewhere in the solar system, on the planet Mars to be precise, stands a far larger and higher peak. Olympus Mons is a massive volcano over 500km in diameter. It stands 22,000m high – almost 2½ times the height of Mount Everest and more than twice the height of Mauna Kea.

Einstein failed maths at school.
TRUE or FALSE?

FALSE! Einstein did NOT fail maths at school.

Albert Einstein was the 20th century's most famous scientist. His groundbreaking work on matter, energy, time and space transformed what we know about the universe. He won a Nobel Prize for Physics in 1921, and was named *Time* magazine's 'Person of the Century'.

Einstein was born in 1879 and went to school in Munich, Germany. By the age of 11 he had conquered college-level physics and was brilliant at maths.

So where did this slice of fake news come from? Well, at age 16 Einstein sat a multi-subject exam for students older than him and did not pass, but this was due to low marks in French and geography, not maths.

The following year, his school's grading system was turned upside down so that a six became the highest grade (it had been the lowest). Einstein's report card that year included sixes in algebra and geometry. Not a fail, but excellent marks!

An NBA basketball player once scored 100 points in a single game.

TRUE or FALSE?

TRUE! An NBA basketball player once scored 100 points in a single game.

Many basketball games end with scorelines of 90–84 or 88–76, but imagine a game in which just one player out of a team scored 100 points all by themselves! The great Wilt 'The Stilt' Chamberlain did just that, playing for the Philadelphia Warriors against the New York Knicks in 1962. Chamberlain scored 41 points in the first half of the game and 59 in the second, averaging a point every 28.8 seconds. It

was an incredibly successful season for Chamberlain as he averaged an amazing 50.4 points per game – still the record.

A blue whale's tongue can weigh as much as an elephant.
TRUE or FALSE?

The largest-ever snake weighed as much as a car.

TRUE or FALSE?

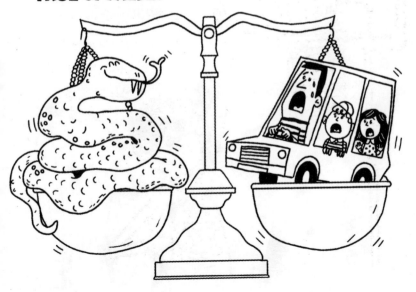

TRUE! A blue whale's tongue can weigh as much as an elephant.

At around 2.5–3 tonnes a blue whale's tongue weighs as much as a female African elephant. For its huge size the blue whale has a surprisingly small eye (about the size of a grapefruit) and throat. It also cannot swallow anything bigger than a beach ball. It gets round this by feasting on tiny shrimp-like creatures called krill continuously – up to 3.6 tonnes of them each day.

The blue whale's tail is also as wide as a set of football goalposts, whilst its heart is about the size of a smart car. The whole creature can reach 30m long – just one metre shorter than a Boeing 737 jet airliner. A typical large blue whale can weigh 140 tonnes, which is approximately the weight of 20 *T. rex* dinosaurs!

TRUE! The largest-ever snake weighed as much as a car.

The fossilised remains of a snake that lived 58–60 million years ago were discovered in Colombia in 2009. Named *Titanoboa cerrejonensis*, the prehistoric snake measured over 13m long and was more than 3.3m round the widest part of its body.

Scientists estimated that *Titanoboa* weighed around 1,100–1,200kg – as much as a hatchback car, or more than an entire class of eight-year-old schoolchildren.

A newborn baby red kangaroo is small enough to fit in a teaspoon.
TRUE or FALSE?

Queen Elizabeth II is a trained truck mechanic.
TRUE or FALSE?

TRUE! A newborn baby red kangaroo is small enough to fit in a teaspoon.

Red kangaroos are Australia's largest marsupials. They can grow up to 1.8m tall, have a 1.2m-long tail and weigh as much as 90kg – heavier than many adult humans. Yet they begin life incredibly titchy: born measuring only 2cm long and able to curl up in a teaspoon with ease.

A baby red kangaroo, or joey, is born weighing as little as one gram, about the weight of a single raisin. They spend months living in and out of a pouch on the front of their mother's body as they grow and develop. The feet and head of a larger joey can sometimes be seen hanging or dangling out of its mother's pouch.

TRUE! Queen Elizabeth II is a trained truck mechanic.

Before she became Queen, Princess Elizabeth enrolled in the military during World War II. She was trained to change tyres, fix trucks and drive them. Another amazing fact about the Queen is that despite having visited more than 110 countries, she does not have a passport!

One man's blood saved the lives of over two million people.

TRUE or FALSE?

TRUE! One man's blood saved the lives of over two million people.

Australian James Harrison nearly lost his life at the age of 14. During a major chest operation, surgeons had to remove one of his lungs and give him many litres of blood to keep him alive. Harrison vowed to donate blood regularly as soon as he was old enough to. True to his word, he donated his first pint (568ml) of blood on his 18th birthday and repeated the process almost every week after that.

Doctors noticed something unusual – his blood contained rare antibodies that combatted a disease called rhesus, which causes a mother's blood cells to attack the cells of her unborn baby. Doctors were able to create a life-saving medication called Anti-D from Harrison's blood.

In 2018, Harrison gave his 1,173rd and final donation at the age of 81. His blood had helped saved the lives of more than 2.4 million Australian babies.

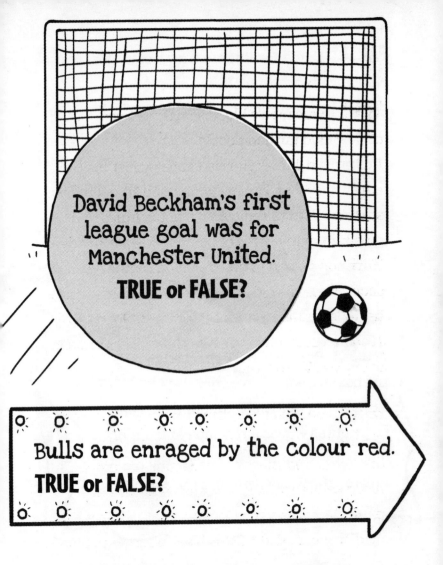

David Beckham's first league goal was for Manchester United.
TRUE or FALSE?

Bulls are enraged by the colour red.
TRUE or FALSE?

Penguins cannot jump.
TRUE or FALSE?

FALSE! David Beckham's first league goal was NOT for Manchester United.

It was for Preston North End, where in 1995 the soccer superstar went on a month's loan from Manchester United. Beckham scored two goals for Preston before returning to United for whom he played over 390 games and scored 85 goals.

FALSE! Bulls are NOT enraged by the colour red.

Bulls are actually colour-blind. When a bullfighter waves a red cape in front of a bull, the animal is irritated or angered only by the movement, not the colour.

FALSE! Penguins CAN jump.

Penguins cannot fly, but they can jump. Adélie penguins can leap out of the water and on to ice or land, leaping up to 2m high.

Chameleons always change colour to blend in with their surroundings.
TRUE or FALSE?

Butterflies taste food with their feet.

TRUE or FALSE?

FALSE! Chameleons do NOT always change colour to blend in with their surroundings.

Chameleons can change colour, often quite dramatically and quickly, but it's rarely for the purpose of camouflage. Scientists think chameleons mostly change colours to attract a mate, to show what mood they're in or to warn other chameleons away.

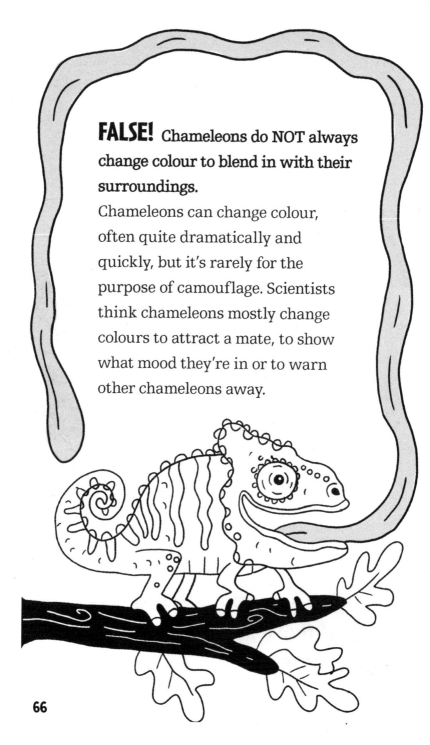

TRUE! Butterflies taste food with their feet.
Butterflies don't have mouths, so their taste buds or taste receptors are on their feet – or, to be more scientific, their tarsi, which is the name given to the last segments of their legs. These receptors detect different chemicals so that a butterfly can identify and feed on a plant's sugary-sweet liquid, nectar.

Female butterflies also use their sense of taste to decide whether a particular place is suitable for them to lay their eggs.

The term 'Fake News' was voted Word of the Year in 2017.
TRUE or FALSE?

TRUE! The term 'Fake News' was voted Word of the Year in 2017.

In 2017, Collins Dictionary announced its Word of the Year. From the more than four billion words and phrases they looked at 'fake news' was chosen as its use rose more than 360 per cent in 2016 and 2017. Some people think that the term was first used on US TV news in the early 2000s, but researchers have found American newspapers from way back in the 1890s with 'fake news' in their headlines.

Goldfish have three-second memories.
TRUE or FALSE?

You have five senses.
TRUE or FALSE?

FALSE! Goldfish do NOT have three-second memories.

No one knows where the rumour that goldfish have super-short memories came from but it's fake. In 2008, scientists trained goldfish to recognise a certain sound and associate it with feeding time. Five months later, the fish recognised the sound, swimming up to get food.

FALSE! You do NOT have five senses.

Your senses gather information about you and your surroundings and send it back to your brain, which analyses the data to make decisions. People have the five senses of touch, taste, smell, hearing and sight, but have many others as well.

These include your sense of balance, temperature, pain, hunger and thirst, and even the sense of knowing where all the parts of your body are without looking at them.

All the cows in the world produce enough gas to inflate 150,000 airships every day.

TRUE or FALSE?

The 'missing link' between apes and humans was discovered in England.

TRUE or FALSE?

More tigers live in the United States than can be found in the wild throughout the world.

TRUE or FALSE?

TRUE! All the cows in the world produce enough gas to inflate 150,000 airships every day.

There are around a billion cows on the planet and each can produce 500 litres of methane gas every day from burping, farting and their manure. This adds up to enough to inflate thousands of airships.

FALSE! The 'missing link' between apes and humans was NOT discovered in England.

Between 1912 and 1914 fragments of a skull and jawbone were dug up in Piltdown, England. The exciting find seemed to show an ancestor of humankind more than 500,000 years old. Piltdown Man was described as the 'missing link' between apes and humans.

But in the 1950s scientists discovered that he was a hoax created using the skull of a medieval person that was only around 500 years old, a jawbone from an orang-utan and teeth from chimpanzees!

TRUE! More tigers live in the United States than can be found in the wild throughout the world. The number of tigers living in the wild has sadly plummeted in the last 100 years. There are now fewer than 5,000 in Asia. In contrast, there are an estimated 7,000 tigers living as pets or in zoos in the United States.

A man has been driving his taxi backwards for over 15 years.
TRUE or FALSE?

Velociraptors were taller than adult humans.
TRUE or FALSE?

TRUE! A man has been driving his taxi backwards for over 15 years.

Harpreet Devi's taxi got stuck in reverse gear in Bhatinda, India, in 2003 and he didn't have the money to fix it, so he carried on driving in reverse … and has done so ever since! In 2005, he drove in reverse from his home in India to Pakistan to promote peace between the two countries.

FALSE! Velociraptors were NOT taller than adult humans.

This myth was made popular by the *Jurassic Park* movies, but in real life *Velociraptor* skeletons revealed these dinosaurs were about the size of a turkey, and only stood 50cm tall.

A mouse can squeeze through a tiny hole made by a ballpoint pen.
TRUE or FALSE?

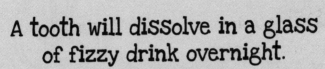

A tooth will dissolve in a glass of fizzy drink overnight.
TRUE or FALSE?

People were once sent places by post, as it was cheaper than travelling by train.
TRUE or FALSE?

FALSE! A mouse can NOT squeeze through a tiny hole made by a ballpoint pen.

But it's only just false. Make the hole a little bigger, about 1.5cm wide, and most mice could find a way through. Mice can even dislocate their jaws in order to squeeze through very tight spaces.

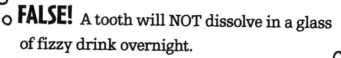

FALSE! A tooth will NOT dissolve in a glass of fizzy drink overnight.

Most fizzy drinks do contain some acids such as citric acid and phosphoric acid, but usually at lower levels than orange juice. These acids can dissolve tooth enamel slowly, but only over a long period of time.

TRUE! People were once sent places by post, as it was cheaper than travelling by train.

When the US Parcel Post system was launched in 1913 some penny-pinching parents figured out it was cheaper to post their son or daughter than put them on a train or stagecoach.

Five-year-old Charlotte May Pierstorff from Grangeville, Idaho, was posted to her grandmother just over 100 kilometres away. Her parents bought 53 cents' worth of stamps and attached them to the girl's coat along with a label saying 'baby chick' and the address she was to be sent to. May travelled the whole way in a mail train's wagon and was then walked to her grandmother's home by a mail man.

A man called Hoover invented the first vacuum cleaner.
TRUE or FALSE?

FALSE! A man called Hoover did NOT invent the first vacuum cleaner.

The first vacuum cleaner was built by British engineer Hubert Cecil Booth in 1901. It was so big that it had to be moved around town by horse-drawn wagon.

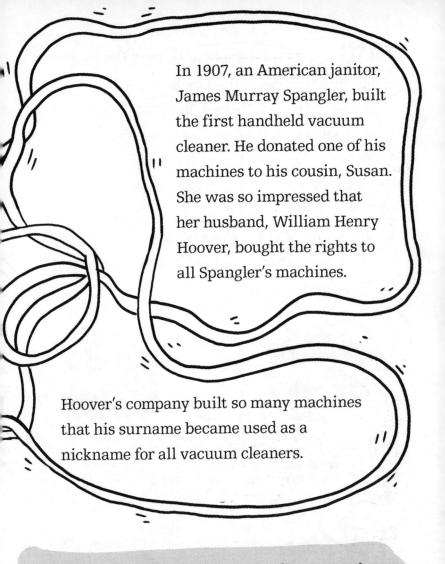

In 1907, an American janitor, James Murray Spangler, built the first handheld vacuum cleaner. He donated one of his machines to his cousin, Susan. She was so impressed that her husband, William Henry Hoover, bought the rights to all Spangler's machines.

Hoover's company built so many machines that his surname became used as a nickname for all vacuum cleaners.

Apollo astronauts were the first living things to reach the Moon.
TRUE or FALSE?

FALSE! Apollo astronauts were NOT the first living things to reach the Moon.

Neil Armstrong and Edwin 'Buzz' Aldrin were the first people to set foot on the Moon, way back in 1969, but they weren't the first living Earthlings to get there. That honour goes to a pair of tortoises, some algae, small worms and bacteria. They all travelled for 6.5 days in space in 1968 in a Soviet spacecraft called Zond 5, and made it safely back to Earth.

A top league football match ended with the score 149-0.

TRUE or FALSE?

Swallowed chewing gum takes seven years to digest.

TRUE or FALSE?

A pigeon-guided missile was tested during World War II.

TRUE or FALSE?

TRUE! A top league football match ended with the score 149–0.

It happened in a play-off match for the National Championship in Madagascar in 2002 between AS Adema and Stade Olympique de l'Emyrne (known as SOE for short).

As a protest at refereeing decisions in an earlier game, SOE scored an own goal straight away. In football, the team that lets in a goal restarts the game by kicking off. So, SOE restarted the game and scored another own goal ... and another ... and another. The game continued like this until at the final whistle, AS Adema had notched up a world record football thrashing ... without even trying!

FALSE! Swallowed chewing gum does NOT take seven years to digest.

Your body absorbs flavourings and sugars in the gum in a couple of days but the chewy base is not digested – it passes right through you!

TRUE! A pigeon-guided missile was tested during World War II.

A prototype missile guided by three pigeons in its nose cone was developed by the United States in the 1940s. Pigeons were trained to peck at a screen when they saw the target. As the pigeons pecked, a cable attached to their heads would move fins on the missile's body to help steer it towards its target. Fortunately for the pigeons the missile was never used with real live explosives!

A bear served in battle with the Polish army during World War II.
TRUE or FALSE?

TRUE! A bear served in battle with the Polish army during World War II.

In 1942, Polish soldiers in Iran befriended a young orphaned Syrian brown bear and named him Wojtek.

The soldiers, from the 22nd Artillery Company, loved the bear. He play-wrestled with them, was taught to salute and even mimicked the soldiers' marching by walking along on his hind legs.

Wojtek was made a private in the Polish army and accompanied the soldiers as their wartime operations took them around Syria, Palestine, Egypt and Italy. During the Battle of Monte Cassino in Italy in 1944 the bear served bravely, unafraid of the explosions and gunfire as he carried food and supplies to soldiers.

Wojtek was promoted to corporal after the battle and the Artillery Company's badge was changed to a bear carrying a large gun shell.

If all Earth's history was squeezed into a single year, King Henry VIII ruled England just 3½ seconds before midnight on New Year's Eve.

TRUE or FALSE?

TRUE! If all Earth's history was squeezed into a single year, King Henry VIII ruled England just 3½ seconds before midnight on New Year's Eve.

You have to remember that Earth has been around a long, long time, around 4.54 thousand million years. Squeezing all that time into a single year, which equals roughly 144 years every second and 8,640 years every minute, yields some surprising results.

Plants on land didn't appear until November, whilst the first four-legged land creatures arrived at the start of December. *T. rex* didn't even make it by Christmas, arriving on Boxing Day. Later that day, a large asteroid from space crashed into Earth and all the dinosaurs died out.

As for King Henry VIII, he reigned between 1509 and 1547 – a period lasting just over a quarter of a second in our squeezed timescale.

Everything expands as it gets hotter.
TRUE or FALSE?

FALSE! NOT everything expands as it gets hotter. You're often taught this fact in science class. Heat a metal, or most materials, and it increases in size to take up more space. It is why the Eiffel Tower, made of iron, can grow up to 15cm in height on the hottest days of the year.

This principle is called thermal expansion, but not every material plays by the rules. Materials made of very long chains of molecules, such as rubber, sometimes curl up and shrink in size when heated.

China used more cement in three years than the United States did in the whole of the 20th century.

TRUE or FALSE?

Caesar salad is an ancient dish named after Roman ruler Julius Caesar.

TRUE or FALSE?

Sunsets on the Red Planet are blue.

TRUE or FALSE?

TRUE! China used more cement in three years than the United States did in the whole of the 20th century.

The United States is the home of big buildings and big cities, and during the 20th century a huge 4.05 billion tonnes of cement were used to build them. However, China used around 6 billion tonnes in just three years – 2011, 2012 and 2013 – as its fast-growing cities sprawled.

FALSE! Caesar salad is NOT an ancient dish named after Roman ruler Julius Caesar.

Caesar salad is thought to have been invented in 1924 in Mexico by an Italian chef, Caesar Cardini, who ran a restaurant in the Mexican town of Tijuana.

TRUE! Sunsets on the Red Planet are blue. Mars appears red to us on Earth due to all the iron oxide in the rock, sand and dust that covers the planet. But some of the dust in its atmosphere blocks much of the yellow and red light from reaching its surface, allowing blue light through, leading to dramatic blue sunsets.

The first president of the United States, George Washington, had wooden false teeth.
TRUE or FALSE?

In the 18th century a chess robot beat Benjamin Franklin and Napoleon.
TRUE or FALSE?

FALSE! The first president of the United States, George Washington, did NOT have wooden false teeth.

Washington suffered with bad teeth throughout his life but he never wore wooden ones. When he became US president in 1789 he only had one of his own teeth still in place, so he had many different sets of false teeth made. Some featured gold, lead and human teeth. Others were carved from the ivory and bones of an animal called a sea horse, which we now know as a hippopotamus.

FALSE! An 18th-century chess robot did NOT really defeat Benjamin Franklin and Napoleon.

In 1770, a mechanical man dressed in robes and turban wowed the court of Empress Maria Theresa of the Austro-Hungarian empire. Its inventor, Wolfgang von Kempelen, claimed he had built a chess-playing automaton (or robot) that could beat all but the very best human chess players.

'The Turk' defeated dozens of chess players all around Europe, including the French leader

Napoleon Bonaparte and American statesman Benjamin Franklin. When people challenged von Kempelen to open the cabinet that sat in front of the automaton, all that was revealed was a maze of gears and levers.

But in the end it turned out that a fake panel inside the desk hid a human chess master who could see the positions of the chess pieces via small magnets.

Fortune cookies come from China.
TRUE or FALSE?

The first known boomerangs came from Australia.
TRUE or FALSE?

Children everywhere are drinking dangerous dihydrogen monoxide.
TRUE or FALSE?

FALSE! Fortune cookies do NOT come from China.

In Japan, fortune-telling sentences on strips of paper became popular in the 19th century. But the familiar cookies, baked with the paper strip inside, were first served in Japanese and Chinese restaurants in California, USA!

FALSE! The first known boomerangs did NOT come from Australia.

The oldest-known boomerang was found in a cave in Poland in 1987. It is made from the tusk of a woolly mammoth and is thought to be about 23,000 years old.

TRUE! Children everywhere are drinking dangerous dihydrogen monoxide.

In 1994, several Internet websites began publicising a colourless, odourless substance that was a major ingredient of acid rain and could be deadly. This dangerous substance is actually good old water (which is deadly if you drown in it!).

Each water molecule is made up of two atoms of hydrogen (*di*hydrogen) and one atom of oxygen (*mon*oxide) so this scary-sounding chemical name, shortened to DHMO, was just another way of saying H_2O!

Spaghetti was shown growing on trees in a BBC TV documentary.
TRUE or FALSE?

TRUE! Spaghetti was shown growing on trees in a BBC TV documentary. In 1957 viewers in Britain were astonished to watch Swiss farmers gathering in their annual spaghetti harvest – from trees! It was on the BBC's serious current affairs programme *Panorama*, so people believed it. Back then, people in Britain were not so familiar with pasta, and many asked the BBC where they could buy spaghetti trees.

People should have spotted the date – the film was shown on 1 April, or April Fool's Day. It was a hoax! Of course, not everyone was fooled. Would you be?

Next time you read an incredible story, ask yourself … is it amazing but true or could it be **FAKE NEWS?!**